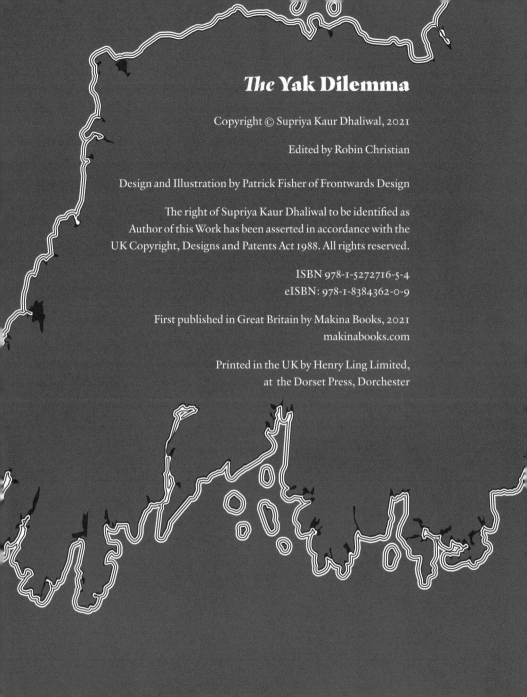

The Yak Dilemma

ISBN 978-1-5272716-5-4
eISBN: 978-1-8384362-0-9

First published in Great Britain by Makina Books, 2021
makinabooks.com

Printed in the UK by Henry Ling Limited,
at the Dorset Press, Dorchester

The Yak Dilemma

Supriya Kaur Dhaliwal

III

IV

I

Meet me in the morning on no man's land

Meet me in the morning on no man's land where there are no magpies, no ravens, no candles, no kettles, no cups, no saucers, no sun, no moon, no light, no darkness, yet it is morning but mornings on no man's land are different from the casual mornings we wake up to.

Meet me in the morning where our heads float and so do our hearts; where there is no gravity and the only thing that keeps us grounded is the fact that we are together and it is that time of the morning.

Meet me in the morning when I will whisper those floating words into your ears; words that will float in the air but you will float to catch them and I will end up chasing you, floating like those bubbles in the beer we drank last night.

Meet me in the morning
on no man's land where our skins
lose their colour; where we are
not white nor brown or black
but just the shade of our most
loved colour. I will be lilac and you
can be that shade of yellow
you like. Everyone will qualify
to be a person of colour.

Meet me in the morning
and come as the image of an image
I have of you, hand over hand,
knee over knee. In that bleeding
memory, our bodies are countries
we trespass to walk from yes to
yes. You convince me if we can
substitute an ampersand for
a comma then it belongs there.

Meet me in the morning
on no man's land. We will create
a daisy chain of ampersands
on no man's land.

Undesigning K-25, Hauz Khas

for Amrita and Imroz

The autocorrect tells me Waris is not spelt so,
        it must be *war is*.

But that is what it has come to now, it is war
        in our homes;

in your home too—every inch of its walls bedecked
        in love and 'bulldozed dreams':

the newspaper headlines
        in disguise.

These walls were so thin that the entire world listened
        in awe

to the many stories that were birthed here: Faiz's ghazals
        in the language

of their Panjab, a mushaira from his country, where,
        in retrospect

Waris Shah lived, who could never speak from his gave
        in solidarity

for this rubble. As the passers-by on the street
        in Hauz Khas

continue to watch these semi-treacherous activities
        in shame—

they put off the thought of repainting the peeling paint
        in a hazel blue

for their walls, just as you did.

An Accidental Sonnet

Wishing to be an ugly and inexpensive
museum artefact, all summer I wanted
to stop writing poems—weighing
the aesthetic pleasure derived
from poems against the things
people are reluctant to look at.
The elderflowers were early this year
but no champagne was made at home
because I was busy waiting for wisterias
to smell like wisterias. Maybe, to be
beautiful is burdensome / and to be
ugly is like being under renovation.
You know, when I say pleasure,
I can't always differentiate it from pain.

Roses for Karl Marx

wrapped in hessian
and taken to the Highgate Cemetery
where the gardens are well-tended
but the living appear to be lonelier
because the dead outnumber them
in their exclusive territory
where you paid £3 to enter

Siri how do I get to Marx's grave
from Eliot's grave

Siri not available
You are not connected to the Internet

Room in Edinburgh

I look at you like I look at a mountain. I never understand the geometry of a mountain—the minute and vast distances between its several folds. If one looks at a mountain long enough, it might appear as something one knows by heart / like I know your face. I have archived each curve of your smile, each flicker of your eye, each line on your forehead for every time your face would not be across mine. God forbid, there shall not be many days like that. Every time one looks at a mountain, a new testimony awaits. Some say that looking at a same mountain twice is equal to looking at two different mountains. The mountain, however, stays in the same place. It could even be immortal. We stay in the exact same place—our own kingdom of mountains. In this kingdom, while we listen to Sinéad O'Connor sing *Drink Before the War* and let our eggs burn, the seagulls hover over the seven hills of Edinburgh—preying on pigeons in the pewter sky. In this kingdom, we hold hands, we kiss, and everything still is bright even in the season that withers everything away.

No One Wants to Think of Marigolds in September

Most passengers who alighted from the train
walked into the other direction as I sheltered

myself from the rain, and the hullabaloo
of the pre-autumnal madness—the pumpkin spiced

pleasures in Starbucks, the squawking of birds
preparing for winter migration and the busker

seeking validation for his terrible cover of Bowie's
Space Oddity. Near the red light at the intersection

with Moorgate Street, a young man handed me
a flyer for *two-for-one* cocktails in a nearby pub

which was called *The Swan & Hoop*
once upon a time, where Keats was born.

These immortal poets are unthinkable
in London rain except in the vicinity of the houses

that mark their birth or death; where their pain
and delight become products of our imagination.

While I got lured by a flyer advertising day drinking
with Keats's ghost, somebody tripped over a bed

of soggy marigold petals, certain that they offered
no sense of harm. It was September after all—

when flowers, even the ones without a murky past
like lifeless nomads, belong only to the ground.

Arabic Lessons

As-salamu alaykum. Peace be upon you.
Wa-alaykumu s-salam. And peace be upon you, too.
We were ten strangers scattered in a seminar room
in a university in Belfast. Our teacher asked us
why were we there. I said I grew up in India
around people who spoke Urdu fluently
and thought I might be able to pick up Arabic quickly.
You know, it is that sort of thing, I want to read
Mahmoud Darwish's poetry in his mother tongue
and live in Beirut, Cairo, Kuwait without having to bargain
for chandeliers or dates; without letting anyone know
I am a foreigner. *So, you are not a journalist*. No, I am a poet.
How long have you lived in Northern Ireland? A few months.
He laughed. For ten weeks, ten of us sat
once a week in the same seminar room waiting
for Arabic to come to us naturally. Ma-Issalama.
Goodbye. Nothing came more naturally than the phrase
for bidding farewell, our minds ready to depart
wherever we had come from.
                              Ma-Issalama.

II

For Vincent van Gogh;
from Q-Park, Museumplein

I have tried to dream that the colour of the moon
is a cross between zinc yellow and chrome yellow,
not just in Vincent van Gogh's *The Starry Night*

but outside the realities of post-impressionism as well.
However, I do not know how to make myself remember
my dreams, to monitor the dosage of yellow in them.

During the summer of 2017, I lived in Borgerhout, Antwerp
in the same neighbourhood as Vincent van Gogh and waited
for metaphors, to shoehorn them into this poem. That summer

everything was yellowed with a tint of ochre – a symptom
of a more general malaise. Several men were seen loafing
about the streets to stub their cigarette butts on bare shoulders.

A man stood naked in his apartment window that overlooked mine
and masturbated. Another naked man who considered himself dandy
enough, sat by his pungent yellow window in *sukhasana*, with his MacBook

resting on his penis. Polaroid pictures were filtered with a fine sepia tone
for archival purposes. Novels of average yet sad millennial romances
were being read with great comfort while the passengers

aboard the Charleroi Airport Coach cringed at the sight of garbage
tourists, who did not impress them with their foreign
language skills. Every unfamiliar word pierced them like a bullet

launched from a toy gun. A teenage boy holding a map anointed
with notes asked me something in German that I could not comprehend.
I assumed if he was in the hood, he must be looking for Van Gogh's

room. There was nothing else worth designating on a map
in this area. I fed him false information with my finger
pointing back in the direction I had come from. *Danke*. My friend

who kindly received me from the train station shushed me
when I said it really looked like a melancholic Beckett novel.
It was autumn by the time I found my way towards Museumplein.

What month do sunflowers die? September. Things were starting to die –
calling cards, lovers, lunch breaks, the ozone layer, sunflowers.
The popsicle seller preferred not to make an appearance anymore.

Outside Rijksmuseum, schoolchildren queued against their will.
One of them called a bully a bully. Once, when a child called the six-year-old
me an ugly duckling, I did not call him a bully. I asked him if the duckling

was yellow. They are not the big things like the apocalypse, cancer
or snakes that intimidate me as much as having to answer back a bully.
In the nearby Q-Park, I shielded myself against the rows of neatly parked cars

holding an *Irises* postcard. On my return to the real world, autumn
had brought rain for the yellow on the ground;
yet no stars.

[This Walled Wasteland]

We looked at the walls. Slabs of concrete symmetrically arranged. Your hands clutching your forearms. Your fingers digging deep into the flesh as if you wear your skin like an elastic sheet. Walls stiff like your shoulders. Walls (un)necessary like vestigial organs. The media has come for the walls. Cameras & microphones waiting for the walls to speak. We are in some wasteland. We are looking at the walls as the walls are looking at us. Walls wanting to wait until the waiting subsides in this two-dimensional reality. Our bodies cemented to the ground as the walls are. How will we find this walled wasteland on a map? We are standing between the walls as if the walls are holding us. We try to please the walls to hold us. What if the distance between the walls is minimising? What if the distance is soon reduced to an arm's length? We cannot anticipate the walls merging. The cameras & microphones cannot anticipate the walls merging. The walled wasteland will be reduced to nothing if the walls merged. We will be reduced to nothing with a single touch if these walls merged. We are still nothing for these walls. Sometimes, it is indeed better if we are not touched.

The Yak Dilemma

While learning what different animals
were supposed to be called, the first kind
of animal I learnt to name was a yak.
My nanny whom I am told was from
Chamba, took the yak business quite
seriously. She made sure I knew we were
no *flatlanders*. Whenever I draw a line
on the paper, I think of her telling me that this line
is River Ravi around which several yaks graze.
Somewhere between learning about
yak milk and yak wool, today I stand
in a labyrinth of questions. In a poetry
workshop in a country with no yaks, I am told
yaks can only be found in Nepal. In another
teahouse setting in the same country, I am told
a yak is a raccoon. Another human contradicts
this notion and adds that a yak is something
like a furry cow often related to the Sherpas
and probably Tibet. I put kibosh on the discussion
before another human tries to venture in
with his own theory of Himalayas and yak meat.
Like the snowflakes from colourless skies
that fall like bullets ricocheting in a war
zone, kissing February's hopeless
grounds, I often wonder—
where have I truly come to?

your bird/my bird

Counted Punjab's fewer than five rivers for days—
their banter like a lost love's show, played for days.

All the sources are worth a footnote in essays,
so is the pain that doesn't go away for days

or doesn't go away at all like a fatal migraine.
The skies on our side have been grey for days.

The bulbul on the barbed wire knows nothing
of no man's land. Her claws splay for days

on the razor-wire fence. The telephone cables stay
entangled between poles of decay for days.

The distance between Jhelum and Satluj is a wound's width.
The bulbul circles above it, looking for prey for days.

She greets the woman who named her daughter
Naseeb (destined not to have to pray for days)

with her birdsong. Like our human speech,
her birdsong has been finding its way for days—

in a dictionary that almost belongs nowhere.
The bulbul yearns to exist in dismay for days

on your land/my land. Your bird/my bird:
what would be claimed as hearsay for days?

Poem in which I am an Interloper in an Art Gallery

after An Indian Lady, perhaps 'Jemdanee', Bibi of William Hickey, painted by Thomas Hickey in 1787

While treading on paths that are so foreign, in a city so foreign towards an art gallery so foreign—I least anticipated to stand on the crossroads to meet a woman bedecked in the kind of jewels that were more familiar to me in that foreign room than my own self. I was looking at her and all the paintings in that room and the room adjoining were breathing on me. Even *The Temptation of Adam* joined in. She (perhaps Jemdanee) was dressed in a pink that was not foreign. It was a pink of crushed peonies and powdered rose. It was the colour of the shadow of cherry blossoms. To not (have to) dress like the women who raised us is considered a revolution in itself by many. It is similar to be willing to talk like the women who did (not) want their daughters to not remain silent. The didactic panel by this painting wanted to reassure me that in order to understand this painting, I must try to know who William Hickey is. While I tried to look for the story of their love, I failed to fill in so many blanks. Like, was this Indian lady sitting cross-legged in front of me really Jemdanee? To have a penchant for other people's love stories is like dying a death that was not really ours to die. There is a risk involved in assuming that the hearts that were foreign were traded because you know, if you are a citizen of everywhere, you are a citizen of nowhere; or just foreign.

Talking to Ghazala after The Republic of Ireland voted Yes to Repeal the Eighth Amendment

History clots the blood running in our veins
like the words of a prayer in an ancient language
unconsciously wired in our memory

since childhood. It could cost us the labour
of a lifetime to unlearn them. Ghazala, our skin
colour on the racial spectrum labels us as brown.

The next time you lay supine facing the sun
on the grass rooted in moist soil,
think of the mud as your nearest kin

in this foreign land. Unbeknown to women
who have died here or elsewhere – who lie
buried among the lands that defied them,

whose ashes were scattered in water bodies
that tore through the areas they could not reach
themselves – we have woken up to a miraculous

Monday morning. Hordes of people wearing
Tá badges, *REPEAL* jumpers and *Together for Yes*
merchandise chanted *Savita! Savita! Savita!*

in the courtyard of Dublin Castle with the furious
spirit of sisterhood as soon as the results came in.
Ghazala, times have been hard. We have been made

to nurse our bodies with terrifying stealth –
our reality now an un-anesthetized amputation
of all the broken dreams of the living and dead.

We cannot feel the same pain for the second time.
Human beings are just so lucky like that, aren't they?
To ease this pain, there were thematically fitting desserts

and I saved you a box of *After-Eight*, Ghazala.

Hotel Poem, Fatih, Istanbul

I eat my Turkish breakfast in a plate
that is an imitation of Byzantine mosaics

in the Hagia Sophia. Mehmet, the server, asks me
if home for me is *Alhind*. When I say yes, it is,

he marvels at the grandeur of the Taj Mahal,
where both of us have not been, yet.

Mehmet tells me about the Blue Masjid's six minarets
and asks if the *azaan* here reminds me

of the *azaan* in the Jama Masjid in Dilli.
I admit that I wish I knew

as I have never been to Jama Masjid either.
However, Dilli is nothing like Istanbul.

It does not rain in Istanbul in July
like the way it does in North India.

Here I wake up to a shining view of the Bosphorus
and I sleep to it, feeling the weightlessness of the sea

taking over every night.

Reading Natalia Ginzburg
in East Cork

Words fail me often and so do shoes.
I always keep a pair ready, polished

in an empty suitcase like an air ticket
without a return date / purchased on a whim.

I wear them only on uncomfortable occasions.
For when I am feeling most comfortable, I long

for the worn-out sneakers I have been wearing
every day for hundreds of days;

trusting them the most to keep my feet warm
and dry, to keep my gait pronounced

like an athlete's or a ballerina's. It is too much
to ask for, perhaps from something lifeless

summoned by all the burdens of the living.
At the edge of this forest and the tree-lined

avenues of a city where I have not yet
been able to go—reside some little virtues

and there, we can ask for everything
that the heart needs and there, we will

know that it would have been the best
if we came in our most worn-out shoes.

Sharing a beer with you

is an important vocation for me, more important
than reading Shakespeare or not reading Shakespeare;

more important than writing a poem so moving
that when I read it to you, standing at Edinburgh Castle—

arm in arm with you, with only your eyes to look
into, overlooking the hazy realities of the city—

I would want the loneliest magpie to respond; and I insist,
sharing a beer with you is more important than not writing

the most moving poem of the universe because who am I
to decrystallize honey that is not in our kitchen, making

strangers' hearts quiver if I only really care about one heart
in the whole world, which seems to be yours.

When Frank O'Hara said, 'I look / at you and I would rather look
at you than all the portraits in the world', I felt something

in me soaring with the fury of an airplane looming up
in the dusky cotton candy May sky. You know, don't you,

that I would indeed look at you and I would rather look
at you than all the portraits in the world, partially because you

are so dear to me, partially because I can care about fox turds
in the garden with you with the same passion as the New Keynesian

divine coincidence or García's divine providence, both
shielding us from the ongoing plague in different manners.

What good can Dora Maar or Amrita Sher-Gil really do
to my sensations when only looking at you can wow me

like the sun's first ray after a blizzard or like dew's
subtle touch on a leaf that is still an infant.

And now while the squirrels hop from one tree to another
to meet an unknown lonely bird singing by herself, I finish

this poem sitting on the staircase as I look up pictures
of Adam Smith's grave where we kissed to bring us

some good fortune; waiting for you, and a beer chilling
in the fridge, that you will bring with all the love and luck

that I need in the world.

III

The quickest way to accidentally kill a succulent is to shower it with love and attention

Some things thrive from minor neglect
We are lucky until we are profoundly unlucky
Rewind the happiness, then press delete, don't recollect
'Watchful dereliction': master this art, it's the key

We might think we are pure as Ganges, after washing ourselves
A succulent would rather be absent in this situation
Or prefer to be relocated elsewhere, among the shelves
Where it can't be seen or touched, or examined by palpation

Love a cactus, name it as if naming a love
There are dogs and cats named after humans
Diana, Jack, Joy, Murashka, Rex, etc. – forty names by Pavlov
For forty dogs who fell prey to his ungentle ruins

We can't give a bad review to our cactus for dying young
Interference is death's obsolete mother tongue

Unmapped Cities

after Italo Calvino's Invisible Cities

I

Dorothea. Anastasia. Despina. Fedora.
Zoheide. Marco Polo's cities we know
for their desires—aluminium towers,
spring-operated drawbridges, desert
expanses, caravan routes, concrete canals,
flesh of a golden pheasant, camels
from whose pack hang wine-skins and bags
of candied fruit, date wine, tobacco,
leaves. Men and women stay up all night
here, talking, talking, in a language
that is a work of their own minds.
Their language of discourse being a secret
and its grammar absurd, each word
concealing another word, each desire
taking its form from another and so on.

We sell our desires in a city
where the nights are horrendously long
and whenever the sun decides to shine
in the wee hours of mornings, it wonders
where the hell is it shining. Lust knows
no night, no morning, no sun, no winter,
no summer and it acts better under no special
circumstance. Lust is an elixir
guaranteed to induce desire. Lust is
the underpaid line manager of desire.
Lust is desire's absurd grammar.
In a city where desire is sold like livestock,
does it become the currency of lust?

II

Diomara. Isidora. Zaira. Zora.
Maurilia. Marco Polo's cities we know
for their memories. Kublai Khan wants
to know if Polo's journey always takes
place in the past. Polo reassures him saying,
"Futures not achieved here are only branches
of the past: dead branches." What is it
in a city that must be remembered?
Names of their inhabitants, their voices'
accent, the features of the faces, dates
of battles, constellations, virtues, mineral
and vegetable classifications. Kublai Khan
wanted to believe an empire is a zodiac
of the mind's phantasms or a season lost
in one city to be retrieved in another.

It sounds like it is a city in a past century
but I can reassure you that it belongs
to the future instead. Some people will say
how cool is this language that is not English—
that even a health warning in it looks amazing
on a tobacco packet. On the other hand,
some people will shush you when you talk
in that language that is not English
with a dear friend, in a café whose name
is not in English. Everyone is so scared
as if this new language will be the death
of English. It is uncanny how languages are lost
in one city to be disregarded in another.

Housing Crisis on Raglan Road

During my early teenage years,
when I was old enough to learn big words—
I thought solitude was soltitude. The extra *t* a sword
to cut through a lapsed state of being on one's own. It appears,
maybe, like a briny situation in the mouth that prefers
the taste of days spent alone. Was it solitude's better byword
for a happier state of mind? Was it a watchword
for failed solitude, the worst of all our fears?

In Dublin, on a day as grey as if smeared with pewter,
I think of Kavanagh while walking through Raglan Road
and his poem of the same name. I think of no kin, no suitor.
I think of the debt these houses have owed
to the people who every day in this city seek recruiters
for new jobs with no solitude or soltitude or abode.

Ghazal on Living in a Hotel in Downtown Cairo

Four walls don't make a home or a house—it takes some doing.
Cocooned among four rented walls, I try to assume, how am I doing?

All the hands I've ever held rest with me on the sheets in a hotel
in Downtown Cairo—so, how do you think in Room 214, am I doing?

My cost of living: the tariff of this rented bedroom plus my own silence.
In the lobby I meet a man from Khartoum. *Habibi, ezayek?* Darling, how are you doing?

I drink cardamom spiced coffee with an only mother who tells me her baby is blind
but has a sense of shadows and perfume. I wonder, how he's really doing?

I rest like animals forced in jars of formaldehyde.
Food here is a tasteless affair—in the lunchroom, how am I doing?

I tour the Egyptian Museum to understand the glory of mummification.
Over the Nile, I watch an airplane loom into the sky—how are the mummies doing?

Hal 'ant masrur? Are you happy? The receptionist asks daily and I nod.
I scrub my rot with a white soap—without a costume, how am I doing?

In Belfast, there's a green toothbrush on my sink that I don't have the heart to bin.
I type a text for its bearer, seeing it in my washroom—*how are you doing?*

Trading Himalayan Saffron for Homesickness

It will take us fifty minutes
to reach the nearest airport.

Mom will insist that I sit
in the front seat. Dad will drive.

We will try our best to take care
of the small talk business.

My eyes will twitch with a tear or two
like the wick that is not the correct size

for the candle. The winter's silverware
on the hills won't have corroded yet.

It could take me from six months
to a year to make the journey back.

I know Mom will have secretly packed
enough saffron for me to last a lifetime

yet she will say, "Take some more *kesar*
for the road. We don't know

when we will see you next."

Love in the Time of Diaspora

I

That one time I slipped into the thoughts of someone
I no longer talk to, my stream-of-consciousness monologue
    was bound to develop a cinematic feel. The correct blue

        of the Dublin sky, how I bypassed Camden Street
            every time to meet you half-way across the Centra
        for proper pints at the Cobblestone or Oscars',

    the same Sixto Rodriguez track playing as the background score
on repeat for every time we walked over that one bridge
    over the Liffey in all her moods and our moods, drifting quickly

        from the north side of the Arran Quay to the south—
            Sugar man, won't you hurry/cause I'm tired of these scenes and
        the fuss of the post-work coffees in Smithfield

    where we would later return each other our books,
as if ceremoniously handing back the burden
    with a tome of Heidegger—it is only yours to deal with now.

II

      That one-pot duck recipe I could never reproduce
in my kitchen, that one business card I could never
         throw away because you sliced a dollop of cheese with it,

             the kind that stank the room out. You quoted Edward Said's
                  definition of Orientalism like a parrot that could cram
             only one sentence. No variety there. We knew this love

      in the time of diaspora could flock to nowhere from here,
for there is no continent where it can flourish.
        We were in the process of becoming displaced lovers

             in the age of displaced postcards for displaced borders,
                  displaced aggression, displaced grief, displaced ovaries.
             When the time came, your neighbours were too busy

        drinking Bloody Marys on their porch,
courtesy of their new hand-blender
        when I walked out for the last time and you,

             you did not care to help me look for my shoes.

In Istanbul

In Istanbul: I dreamt in a language
I understood vaguely, my dream a juxtaposition of
the broken pieces of my half-baked Arabic
& over-ripened Hindi. When the word for Hello
landed on my tongue in Turkish—*mehraba*,
my mouth relished the taste in every crevice
between its each letter: the *m* melting gently
at the rims of my upper and lower lip,
the *e* a muffled shout out of the neck,
the *r* rolling like a pebble I accidently
swallowed, heaving out an *h* in exasperation,
the *–aba*, I call that latter part, like I would
have called my father in Urdu as *abba*.
In Istanbul: I went to a *kitabevi* in Taksim
district. *Kitabevi*, the Turkish for bookstore
appeared subconsciously to me as *kitab devi*
in Hindi, meaning The Goddess of Books.
In Istanbul: where when the water sails
between its two halves, one half becomes
Asian, another European.
In Istanbul: the city of Bosphorus, Tutku
sat across me in Kadiköy drinking beer,
reluctant to share the red-skinned peanuts
with the man who asked for them.
I sat aghast at their drunken stupors.

In Istanbul: when you are there, kindly buy no guidebook to navigate, rely on no scripted monologue. In Istanbul: where Orhan Pamuk dreamt of writing a novel about the city along the lines of *Ulysses*, let the city's *hüzün* (sadness) be yours, let its *mutluluk* (happiness) be yours.

Appointment with Norah Richards

Dressed in black from head to toe
(to look as white as I could)
I arrived in a Himalayan village.
I wore no make-up, my sunken eyes digging deep
into their sockets in jet-lagged miseries—
I still looked very young to look like someone who lives here.
It was raining and I was reluctant to carry an umbrella—
my form of mellow protest against the nature.
As a child, I wanted to venture out as far West
as I could. As an adult, I have come crawling
back to the mountains. I have heard
that writers, actors and theatre practitioners galore
live in Andretta now. However, no one tries
to indulge in small talk with me. They do not like
the artist-kind around here in this Artists' Colony.
There is a famous art gallery around the corner
that I do not enter—loitering in the outskirts
of the famous artist's artistic shadow, like a trespasser.
I came looking for someone else, for something else.

But who is it? What is it?

I have come here as an intruder.

I have come from the land of Lady Gregory
to the land of the Lady Gregory of Punjab
which is my land too, to learn of her mud-house
and her amphitheatre, to learn of pre-partition Punjab—
life in Kangra—for no one knows of her as Irish in Ireland,
she must have found it better here, against the backdrop
of the hills, forests and monasteries. I am here to hunt for the dupatta
that embraced the edges of her temple and to sit in the light of her lantern
refracting the same amount of brightness against the terracotta tinted windowpanes.
I am here, if they ask me, to know what they know of her,
to get familiar with that *familiarity*—
Oh, watchers of Norah's kingdom-land,
"Is she my sister from another century?"
While availing myself a handful of the numerous luxuries
of the universe—living in the Himalayan highlands
definitely topped the not-very-long list. Did it top
Norah's list too? I waited and waited in her amphitheatre
to get an answer. But this is not how you talk to the dead
or to the ones who are eternal, now living in secrecy.

Norah, I will come for you again.

Drinking Coffee Together

Between us
is an almost empty cup
with a lipstick smear—
noir red, the colour
of blackberries soaked
in water for aeons
until the last drop evaporated.
An impression of my lower lip
is patterned on the rim
in its cakey magnificence
like wet sand
on some cold beach
pecks naked feet.
There is some leftover
coffee inside,
lined in circles.
It will be decades
before I understand
coffee's defeat
inside the cup
or between us.
We ticked the boxes,
all the ones that we could
with invisible ink
and everything remained undone.

An ex-boyfriend once
returned me a box
of tampons, not
wanting to keep it
with his soon-to-be-wife's
things nor wanting to pass
them to her. He passed
everything else. I did
not tell him they were
not mine. It matters
what we tell each other.
I do not tell you I do
not love you nor
do you. You order
another coffee.

Migrant Words

for Amarjit Chandan & John Berger

somewhere I cannot now go
I buried some words from my dictionary of lament—
a language I spoke long ago

I have a vain hope they will grow
into a dialect of some hybrid descent
somewhere I cannot now go

sihari (ਿ), bihari (ੀ) and other vowels will plough
a cadence that my anglophone tongue could not invent—
a language I spoke long ago

chicken tikka masala did not originate in Glasgow
someone told me this in my mother's accent
somewhere I cannot now go

when I am asked about my pronunciation of 'th' in Thames and *thug*, I owe
them the words that come to me in Punjabi, to reinvent
a language I spoke long ago

on seeing love being celebrated through every bay window
my eyes bleed counting the years I spent
somewhere I cannot now   go
speaking the language my mother's mother spoke long ago

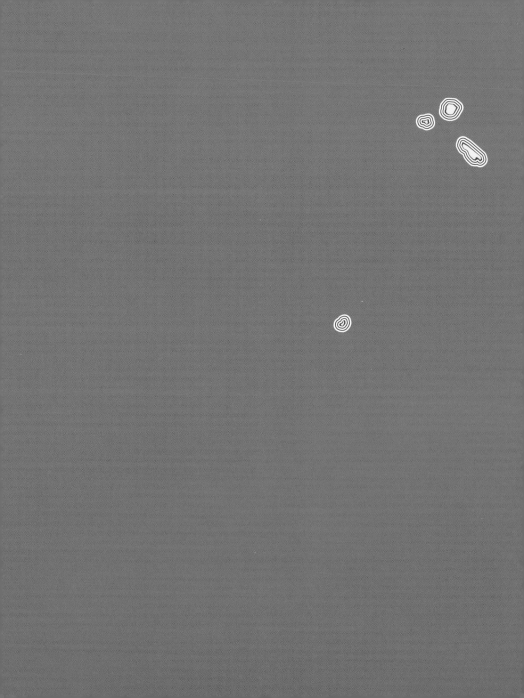

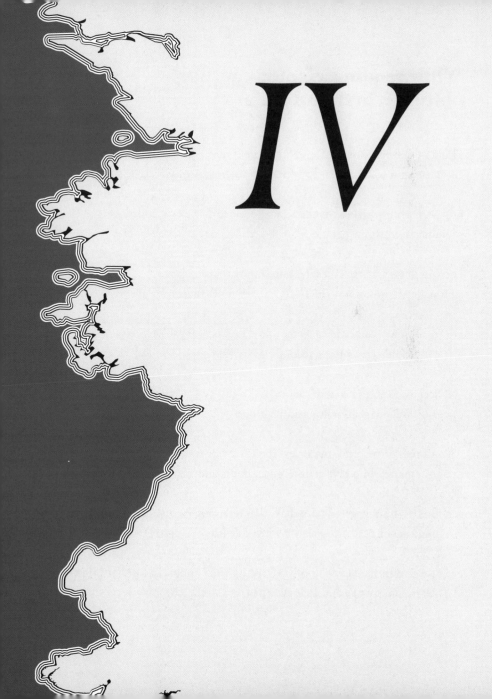

IV

While reading a famous author's obituary, in the afterlife

I hold myself responsible for many misfortunes of the universe—
climate crisis, corruption, demonetisation, homegrown terrorism,

human mobility across the earth labelled as refuge crisis, murders,
prejudice against my people, shushed ethnocentrism, slavery etc.

For years I thought the moon could shine brighter above
a Himalayan mountain. The truth is that a few thousand feet

are absolutely redundant in terms of the units of length in astronomy.
The moon is about 1.3 light-seconds away. That should be 240,000 miles.

While elaborating a broader theory of the galaxy, my high school teacher
once pointed out that looking at the moon while standing on a chair

will not make it appear any closer. The extra boost of the chair
does not make a blind bit of difference. For modernity's sake, I have newer

versions of the fabricated tales that I was fed upon like Peter Pan never left
Kensington Gardens and Snow White hid with the Seven Dwarfs

because they did not own bloody passports and Cinderella lost her slipper
at a ball in Lahore to wake up in Amritsar after it had become

a separate country overnight. Our fairy tales are futile like the lapsed
insurance policies. It is not known where the dead dreams

or even the dead people go, nor it is known why a person
would decide to rest in front of an estate agent's office

while walking their dog. One day, the dead will outnumber
the living on Facebook and we will crash a party hosted by the ones living

in the afterlife.

The women who dine alone, dine alone

I

On my way to a diner on Dame St., I see sixteen-year olds,
                singing Barbie anthem on cobbled paths of Temple Bar,
beer cans in their hands. It was like seeing people seeing films
                in which they wished to be cast as leading actors.

On getting to the diner, I sit with my dinner
                in the first-floor seating area, watch a woman
blow-drying another woman's hair
                inside a third-storey Georgian window, on other side.

II

I finish my food quickly, sit there gathering bits
                for the film I should be writing,
my actor, an Irishman who wants to get through
                the length and breadth of India on trains, only.

His bed on which he sleeps in Dublin
                comes from Ikea and is *Made in China*.
When he watched Titanic at the Odeon in 1997,
                he yelled to himself, "For fuck's sake, SINK!"

My actress has travelled to fourteen countries
        to photograph women who dine alone.
She wants to beat the single-female diner syndrome,
        dining alone, for her, not a *tour de force*.

She dines alone too, in her country, in fourteen countries,
        not having to come home to cats or dogs.
The women who dine alone, dine alone.
        They just do.

III

On my way home, I'm told by a friend
        there is something very English about the way
I hold my cigarette between my fingers.
        I nod but the words get to my blood and bile.

In my dream, his ghost whispers with a lilt of
        Americanness in my ear, correcting my accent.
The following day, I go out wearing the sweet scent
        of cigarette ashes on my sweater.

Table for one, please.

Vulnerability Study

The consonants falling out of your mouth like kernels off a corncob. Feeling hurt in one language to heal in another. Looking for helping verbs in translation to navigate through all the stamps on your passport— your only directory of every desire; bound to fade, expire, renew over time. The vague sense of guilt on plucking a flower or killing an animal for the first time yet experiencing no pain. Feeling the summer's triumph on your skin & winter's defeat in your bones. The memory of every window you looked out of, stirring your vision, blurring your reality. An immigrant saga on the hotel telly. Breakfast buffets. Nothing shared except the toothpaste. Sheets wrinkled like our lives. An investigation into the intimate affairs from yesteryears. A stranger's tongue twirling with words like kismet & karma, to know *where are you originally from*. Standing still like an elevator out of order, so that no human comes closer. Preserving walls with bullet holes to pierce the hearts of the naïve. Hunting for synonyms for an extinct language in a foreign country. Seeing things that are not things but images of things that mean other things. Swallowing words like medicine.

On wearing a Sadri in the West,

you will be told it is a beautiful vest.
You will enlighten the bearer of the compliment
who has never been to your country that this vest—
the cut-sleeved jacket is called a Sadri
and is native to your home state Himachal Pradesh.
You will draft a list of its characteristic features in your mind,
calling it a sad intellectual's jersey or an ageing politician's cape
or a proxy of the Scottish Harris Tweed.
In Ireland, it will be December,
the temperature outside 3 degrees Celsius.
You will get dressed in opaque leggings
to shield your legs from the cold wind,
matching the colour of the brightest petal
on your free-flowing dress.
Your boots will be knee-length and black,
their leather, worn out with each step taken
away from your mountain land.
Your Sadri will not match the pansies on your dress,
or your boots or your leggings.

It will outstand, like you do when you stand
behind the mic to read your Himalayan poem
in a pub in an Irish town and they call you foreign.
The poem will carry a whiff of cosy air
diffused between the crisp creases of a delicately
folded 'pure wool' Kullu shawl.
You will carry that smell of aged wool with your Sadri.
That will be the closest you will be able to get to home,
in the pub, in an almost unknown Irish town.
Your buttoned-up Sadri will hide the extra beer you will drink.
Your Sadri will warm your body full of red meat
and artificial dairy products, but no love.
On the train home, you will see an Indian friend
wearing a Sadri on your Instagram in Dublin,
playing the piano in Pearse Station,
you'll relay the message, "You're rocking the vest,
we call it Sadri in Pahari", our mountainous dialect.
"New word learnt", they will say.
"We call it Bandi in Uttar Pradesh."

The Famous Writer

for Claire Clairemont and Lord Byron,
if they went on a holiday in 2021

The famous writer forgot to pack an extra pair of pants
and had to wait in his underwear for them to dry when he finally
washed them. Their hosts kept bees, goats and lived without the Internet.

The famous writer got angry because a bee stung his nose
and a goat bit his only pair of pants that hung on the washing line
4000 m above the sea level where the ozone layer must be thinning.

The famous writer stood naked on the thatched roof and called it rustic,
declaring this life boho enough and proposing to buy new charpoys for a hut
not theirs, nor a pukka house, knowing this would not last forever. She slyly agreed.

The famous writer made kiwi jam a few years later. He sent her samples
with a note mentioning she should have gone to the forest with him to pick berries
for money. She preserved the note in strong bleach and ate the delicious jam every day

with her toast until she got sick of it.

Room in Palampur

It was a bit like entering the wrong room
in my dream, where I saw you knitting
as you sat on the same bed as the woman
with a neat bob who was talking on the phone.

It could have been an Edward Hopper
painting but I recognised the sheets
and the angles at which the light reflected
in that room. In the same dream, I watched

you sit with my mother as you checked
your email, updated your Facebook friends
with the misdoings of the government etc.
On waking up, I shouted to ask my mother

if you were still in the house, only to realise
that I had woken up in a different house,
in a different country, thousands of miles
away from you and my mother, where

the sheets are new and the light
does not bounce back at familiar angles.

The Architecture of a World-Famous Romance

for Leonard & Marianne

The foundation of this romance lies somewhere
it should not. Its walls are painted with the blue
of the Aegean Sea, to go with the pink

heather that lines the balustrade. Here the longing
for each other hangs like price tags on unworn coats
in the wardrobe, and the waiting is contained

in the neatly folded white linen sheets—not a wrinkle
to bother their quietude. The darlings do not meet
at the windows anymore—the fine square

glass panes of the bay window dividing all the love
there ever was, equally. Spirits of lovers galore
harmoniously hide with their letters in the oak chest

in the attic like a muezzin waiting to announce a prayer call
from the minaret. Some mornings, the seagulls who arrive
in colonies of hundreds can be heard screeching

with anguish—a bleak prophecy of the collapse
of this house of cards. The indoor plants are not dead
yet. A single touch of their bearer could bring them back

to life or take them to their deathbeds. The corners
are crowded with cobwebs—this is now an ancient
cottage on the cusp of decay. Love, here, prefers to live

with the spiders. If either of them loses this home,
they will be left with nowhere to go. The aftercare
of this romance is a lesson that cannot ever be unlearnt

like the skill of using a mortar and pestle. Love, here,
is the warmth of a long nightdress for the cold winters
ahead. It is a rustle, a sigh. It is a nomad's requiem.

Now so long, Marianne, it's time that we began
To laugh and cry and cry and laugh about it all again

Reading Agha Shahid Ali in Northern Ireland

My uncles drink Scotch by the gallon
and my aunts make endless cups of *cha*—
each uncle being the father of a daughter
who lives overseas for a better fortune,

and each aunt being the mother of a son
who immigrated to become *the one
who got away from the mafias
that wanted to get hold of his inheritance.*

When my family sees Kashmir being turned
into A Country Without a Post-Office
on their tellies, wherever they are sipping
their Scotch and *cha*, they call me to tell

the BBC has reported Northern Ireland
as the Kashmir of the United Kingdom. I sigh
when my uncle asks me to spell Belfast, adding
how does he even get here from London?

I should have chosen to study in California
instead, he thinks. Who am I to say anything?
I write ghazals in English in a country
where I am constantly told that English

is not my first language and yet I hide
my pain under iambic pentameter.
When I read my Anglo-ghazal
in a theatre about the partition of Punjab

in front of the best lot of poets around,
someone calls my lot of people *refugees*.
Agha, how little we knew!
We were exiles in every land,

every language, even the language
in which words were unimportant—
when we did not cry in Urdu on our births,
and our last cries that refuse to be in Punjabi—

our only indifferently innocent tributes,
sent out to a world
which was never ours,
which could never be ours.

What Jasmine Said

Jasmine always said April is not the cruellest month.
It is November when it is winter, and we start to put

rum in our bodies as if it is an antifreeze
our organs cannot survive without.

But 2019 is gritty and all about celery juice.
This month is the penultimate act of a twelve-part tragedy

no one wants to buy the tickets for. The show still runs
and I fly out to Cairo to tour the Pyramids of Giza.

At this ancient wonder, the Sphinx is tinier
than I had expected it to be. I lose

half my toenail in an Egyptian sandcastle
and feel like a princess who is not a princess

because she is wearing boots
and they are so fucking tight.

I would like to extend my gratitude to the editors of these
publications where some of these poems first appeared.

The Lonely Crowd, *The Pickled Body*, *Poetry London*, *Seven Responses
by The Lifeboat Press* (in conjunction with the *Metropolitan Arts
Centre, Belfast*), *Ambit*, *The Irish Times*, *Banshee*, *Poetry Ireland
Review*, *Cyphers*, *The Tangerine*, *RTÉ*, *Hello I am Alive: Poetry Ireland
Introductions*, *The Bombay Literary Magazine*, *Madras Courier*, *The
Alipore Post*, *Gutter*.

Acknowledgements

Thanks to my teachers and mentors, Ciaran Carson, Gitanjali Mahendra, Colette Bryce, Nick Laird, Stephen Sexton, Leontia Flynn, for their generosity, and for always telling me what else I could do with a poem or just life, in general.

Thanks to Sakshi Attri, Yashasvika Bhardwaj, for always making sure that home remains for me what home must, and for always reaffirming my faith in home and beyond. Thanks to Dasom Yang, Madeleine Saidenberg, Micaela Rodgers, Aastha Trehan, for always sharing that one last chocolate, one last whiskey, one last cup of tea, one last pastry that would make everything better. Thanks to Marcella Prince, Ellen Orchard, Jake Hawkey, Kelly O'Brien, Charles Laing, Mícheál McCann, Melissa Rutnagar, for a lot of things but mostly for their friendship and kindness.

Thanks to Robin Silas Christian, Patrick Fisher, Jordan Taylor-Jones, for creating this book and nourishing it with the best of everything. Thanks to Emily Cooper, without whom *The Yak Dilemma* would not have been real.

Thanks to my Dad, Yadwinder Singh Dhaliwal, for always seeing the good in everything. Thanks to my departed Mum, Simerjit Kaur Dhaliwal, for always telling me that all that there is in this world could be a poem.

And lastly, thanks to my partner, my lover, my muse, to the only audience that I need in this world, Raman Singh Chhina, for all that there has been, there is and there ever will be.